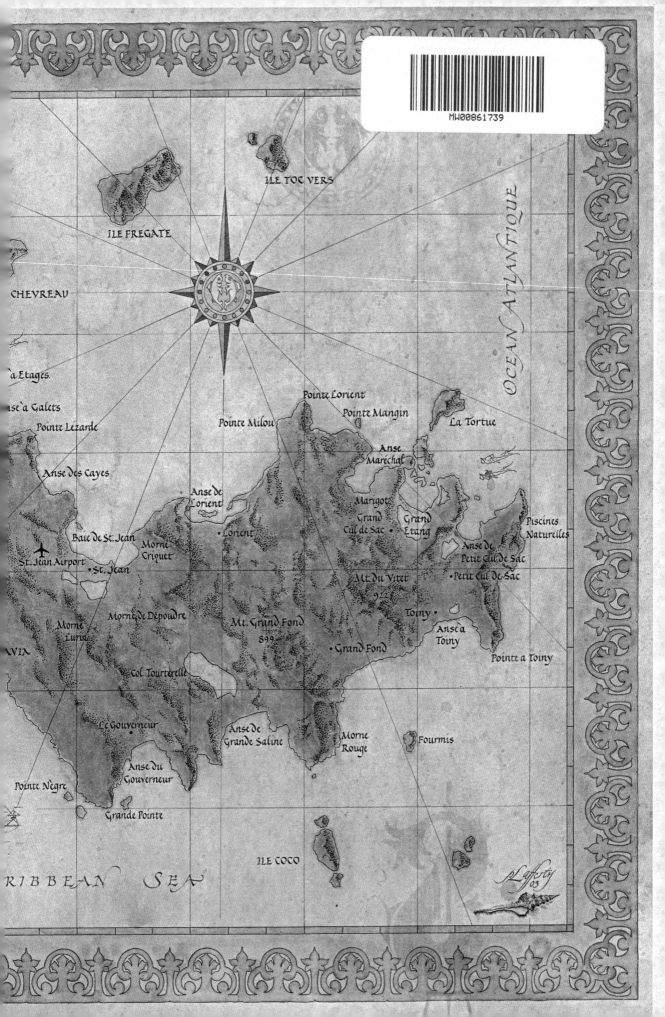

IN THE SPIRIT OF
ST. BARTHS

Text © 2011 Pamela Fiori
© 2011 Assouline Publishing
3 Park Avenue, 27th Floor
New York, NY 10016 USA
Tel: 212-989-6769 Fax: 212 647-0005
www.assouline.com
ISBN: 9782759405176
10 9 8 7 6
Printed in Turkey.

PAMELA FIORI

IN THE SPIRIT OF
ST. BARTHS

ASSOULINE

Contents

An aerial view of St Barths.

Introduction:
An Island Like No Other

The year was 1987. I was on a cruise in the Caribbean on a small luxury liner called *Sea Goddess*. At the time I was editor in chief of *Travel & Leisure* and went on scouting trips frequently—often enough to be discerning, at times skeptical, but never to the point of becoming jaded. For me, there were always discoveries waiting to be made, and the next one was about to come into view. The ship's itinerary is somewhat of a blur, but I clearly remember my final destination: the French West Indies island of St. Barthélemy, commonly called St. Barths, St. Barth (the French name), or St. Bart's (the most common American spelling).

I'd heard about St. Barths, and the magazine had covered it before—as early as 1977, in an article written by the highly respected *New York Times* scribe Tom Wicker. It was a perfectly fine essay, prosaically entitled "St. Bart's." Its subtitle defined the place as "the slow-paced island that warms the weary soul."

There were only two photographs in the layout. One was of the port town of Gustavia. The other showed two female traders selling their wares. It was a misleading image. The women were black, seemingly West Indian, clothed in their native dress and most likely from one of the neighboring islands such as St. Martin, Anguilla, Martinique, or Guadeloupe. Why misleading? Because the truth was, and is, that St. Barths is a mostly white, decidedly French island. This is neither a criticism nor an endorsement, merely a fact.

We set the record straight in 1985, when we sent one of our editors, Malachy Duffy, to the island to write a thoroughly researched and enticingly photographed story that is to this day, in my opinion, one of the best ever done about St. Barths. Mal had been reading about the island to the point of being "absolutely transfixed by the idea of the place." To his credit, he sensed that St. Barths was "ready" in *Travel & Leisure* terms. That meant having all the right ingredients for its readers: a reasonable number of high-end hotels, decent-to-excellent restaurants, an embracing ambiance, and a certain chic.

"As soon as the small plane made its approach," Mal recalled recently, "I was aware that something was different. The traffic is directly beneath you as you land, and the sunbathers on the beach

Previous pages: It takes a skilled pilot to land on the 2,170-foot-long runway without ending up in the Baie de St. Jean.
Opposite: The author shows off a chic pareo on Gouverneur Beach.

seem so close as to be almost touchable. My only Caribbean experiences up to that point were Anguilla and the Virgin Islands. St. Barths was much more sophisticated, yet still casual." Remember, this was more than two decades ago. "The food was great—delicious mussels like I'd never tasted before. The beaches were beautiful. I went back two years ago, and the essence of the island is still the same. The St. Barths of yesterday is the St. Barths of today." Or as another St. Barths habitué who has known it as long as Mal says, *"Plus ça change, plus c'est la même chose"* ("The more things change, the more they stay the same"). Not everyone agrees. There are plenty of residents and frequent visitors who feel that the island has changed dramatically and not entirely for the good, that the "old days" were simpler, safer, easier. More on that later.

Travel & Leisure was hardly the first magazine to recognize the charms of St. Barths. It had been singled out by many publications, including the tony *Town & Country*, in lavish portfolios by none other than Slim Aarons, who made a career out of portraying beautiful people having a wonderful time in enviable places. This was Slim's stock-in-trade, and he did it better than any other photographer in his time or any other. When Slim shot women in glamorous resorts, they had several things in common: They were often blonde, always gorgeous, usually sexily clad in bikinis or sarongs and languorously spread across chaise longues or divans—like odalisques. The females in his St. Barths takes were no exception.

So back to 1987 and my first foray: I disembarked from the ship, went immediately to my hotel—the Manapany—and was led by a flirtatious young French fellow to my room. It was situated right on the beach, so that when I walked out the door, my first step would be into the warm, fine sand. Eager for a dip, I took off my clothes and was about to slip into my swimsuit when in walked the flirtatious young Frenchman carrying a bucket of ice containing a bottle of champagne and two flutes on a silver tray. He was wearing a smile. I was wearing nothing. Well-married woman that I was (and am), and old enough to be his mother, I waved him off, but not without thinking, "Thanks for the compliment."

Sometimes such encounters are more lasting. A divorced woman I know had as her pilot a much younger man (also French) for her plane bound for St. Barths. On her return flight, she had the same pilot. At an opportune moment, he made a pass. She returned the favor. He convinced her to stay overnight in San Juan, where he had to make a stop. "It gave a whole new definition to the expression layover," she said gleefully. Years later, they are still in touch.

If this makes St. Barths sound like a seductive place, it is. The men and women who work on the island are good-looking, in great shape, and not ashamed to show it. The sight of someone half or totally naked on the beach is a common one, and while not every tanned, well-oiled body is camera ready, enough of them are at least pleasing to the eye.

Opposite: A colorful harbor view.

From left to right: A view of the main port, Gustavia; French cuisine at La Case de l'Isle restaurant at Hôtel Saint-Barth Isle de France; a Mini Moke.

St. Barths is also expensive, a circumstance that keeps it in that high-flying zone reserved for the well-to-do. This was true even in 1987. One of the reasons I stopped on the island was to meet up with my friend Dena Kaye, an early St. Barths devotee, who was renting a villa there. She suggested we go to a place for lunch called the Lafayette Club because, she said, "we could eat light, sink our feet into the sand, and be served by really cute waiters." She was right on all counts. As I recall, we each ordered fresh fish and a green salad; no wine, just bottled water. For dessert we shared a plate of strawberries. When I motioned for the check, the cute waiter handed it to me. It was in French francs and the equivalent of $200—and they didn't take credit cards. This was twenty-four years ago. Next to us an acquaintance of Dena's, an American, was hosting a party of six or eight. I could almost hear him gasp when his check arrived. To this day, when he and I run into each other, we laugh about it (although it didn't seem so funny at the time).

Getting around the island back then required renting a Mini Moke, a tiny utility vehicle like a Jeep, but with small wheels and low ground clearance—a sort of beach buggy and certainly not built for steep inclines or going off road. One of the appeals of St. Barths is that it is a volcanic island, with lots of hills and cliffs, rather than a flat coral island. That means

narrow roads, ups and downs, and dangerous curves. Imagine riding on a motorized donkey under such circumstances. Count on a lot of lurching, frequent and startling stalls, and a consistently bumpy ride, all engendering a general sense of heart-stopping terror—and that's in broad daylight. If your taste runs to roller coasters, St. Barths is for you. If not, get thee to Anguilla or the Turks and Caicos.

My husband still has a hard time adjusting to driving on the island, even though today's car rental offerings have vastly improved and you rarely see a Mini Moke (to the regret of those who regard it with cultish adoration). To be on the safe side, and unless you are staying in St. Jean or Gustavia, take a taxi at night, especially if you'll be traveling on unfamiliar roads.

St. Barths has been called the St. Tropez of the Caribbean. Depending on how you feel about St. Tropez, this is either a plus or a minus. There are certainly similarities: They are both resorts whose language, food, and attitude are as French as their penchant for monokinis, pareos, and rosé wines. But because of St. Barths' ninety-four years of Swedish occupation, there is also a subtle tie to that Scandinavian country. Gustavia, the main town, is even named after King Gustav III. The influence, however, is not the prevailing one.

The fact that St. Barths is primarily a white island rubs some people the wrong way. Their objection is that St. Barths is not "authentically" Caribbean or, more specifically, not West Indian, even though it is technically part of the French West Indies and is what is called an "overseas collectivity" of France. There are historical reasons for its population's being chiefly Caucasian that are cited in this book (and elsewhere), and these have more to do with who originally came to the island than with who was kept out. Increasingly, St. Barths attracts a loyal following of prominent African Americans who, having tried other Caribbean destinations, favor this island for the same reasons others do.

As David Matthews, the British-born owner of the Eden Rock hotel, says, "Jane [his wife] and I were comfortable in London and Yorkshire. St. Barths was just what we were seeking. If you want to change your life, as we did, move to France or to a French culture. The French, we learned, are very right about many things."

My own fascination with St. Barths, both professional and personal, continued when I became editor in chief of *Town & Country* in 1993, and we covered it several times in the years that followed. At that point the island was established as the darling destination in the Caribbean. The old rich, like the Rockefellers, had sold their properties, and new money had arrived on the island—hedge funders, pop stars, and, eventually, dot-commers, particularly in high season. Like other islands in the Caribbean, St. Barths weathered some economic downturns, tropical storms, and a ferocious hurricane—and perhaps it did so better than others. As Charles Vere Nicoll, owner of the Hôtel Saint-Barth Isle de France and vicar of the island's Anglican church, puts it: "St. Barths is a tiny bubble at the top end of the market: a little bit of France in the tropics . . . solidly French with a tinge of America. It always went for the high end, never the middle. That is what saved it in the recession."

St. Barths is also appealing because of what it lacks. There are no casinos, no golf courses, no major airport, no high-rise hotels, no water slides for kids, and no other man-made attractions, at least not yet (and those who love it hope not *ever*). Like Capri, another island for which I have a deep affection, it succeeds on its own merits and doesn't try to be anything other than what it is: a rare and resilient beauty. May it always remain so.

Previous pages: Slim Aarons captured Stephan and Stephanie von Watzdorf relaxing by the pool in 1973. Before her marriage, she was Princess of Sayn-Wittgenstein-Berleburg.

St. Barths lures the beautiful and the affluent with its
promise of balmy days, magnificent sea views and soft,
white-sand beaches.

Tropical birds like parrots and macaws add further splashes
of color to life on St. Barths.

The Little Pebble

A tiny barren island barely eight-square-miles, lost in the Lesser Antilles. One of the oldest islands, with a nucleus dating back five million years. From the outset, St. Barthélemy was destined to suffer terrible periods of drought and torrential rains.
Stanislas Defize, painter and filmmaker

The ironic thing about the success of St. Barthélemy is that in its infancy, it had so little going for it. By comparison with other Caribbean islands, it was so small as to be insignificant, dwarfed by St. Martin, Guadeloupe, and Martinique. It was hard to reach (and still is), and its land wasn't exactly arable: It could barely grow anything except cotton and could not sustain a sugar industry, something that helped its neighboring islands. Who could have imagined that little St. Barths would become one of the most desirable destinations on the planet?

Surely not the Arawak Indians, its earliest inhabitants, a primarily agricultural people. Following in their bare footsteps in the twelfth or thirteenth century were the Caribs, who hailed from the north coast of South America. Pushing their way into the Caribbean waters, they invaded several islands. St. Barths was among them, but certainly was not the most important. The Caribs were the opposite of the peace-loving Arawaks. Wielding bows and arrows, they were rumored to be fierce-looking maneaters (though by many counts this practice was related to war, not general cannibalism). For all intents and purposes, St. Barths wasn't "discovered" until the late fifteenth century, and then by none other than Christopher Columbus, who spotted it (but didn't actually land there) when he was returning to Spain from his second voyage to the West Indies. He named the island San Bartolomé after his brother Bartoloméo. But it still "belonged" to the warmongering Caribs, who prevailed over the entire Lesser Antilles. Then came the pirates—some English, some French. If all of this sounds a bit vague, it's that there is little documentation about St. Barths, because most of the profit-making focus was on the other islands, which had far more potential.

It wasn't until the mid-seventeenth century that the island began to form its French roots, in the form of its European settlers, who were mostly from Normandy, Brittany, and Poitou by way of St. Kitts—but not before it was briefly in Spanish hands. Interest in St. Barths ebbed and flowed according to who passed through it and which country was in charge as its guardian. In 1674, Louis XIV decreed

Previous pages: Baie de St. Jean, site of the island's first hotel, the tiny Eden Rock; St. Barths Bucket Regatta, 2010.

that St. Barthélemy was part of the Kingdom of France. According to *The History of St. Barthélemy*, by Georges Bourdin, by 1687 the population "consisted of 501 inhabitants, including 355 whites, 141 slaves and five persons of mixed blood." This dispels the long-held notion that there were no slaves on St. Barths (slavery was eventually abolished, in 1847).

For a long stretch, the St. Bartians were subject to raids, massacres, and general unrest. A period of peace prevailed for about thirty years, starting in 1713 and ending in 1744, when the English seized St. Barths, causing many residents to flee. But as small as the white French population was, they returned and stubbornly remained. One report describes them as "good people, very poor, honest, rather ignorant, and quite quarrelsome."

France maintained control of the island until it was ceded by Louis XVI (Mr. Marie Antoinette) to Sweden in 1785. By then St. Barths had a total population of 739—"458 whites and 281 blacks," according to Bourdin. The main crop was cotton, and the rest of the land consisted of swamps and beaches, so the deal—in exchange for warehouses in the port of Gothenburg, as well as trading rights in the Baltic—was not a big win for Sweden. That same year, the island became a free port, exempt from custom duties—and it remains that way to this day.

The Swedes set about organizing and developing St. Barths, particularly the main port, Gustavia. In 1801, enter the English, who once again took over, but the island reverted to Sweden a few months later—although the English stayed around. Under Sweden, St. Barths grew both in population and in amenities; grocery stores, hotels, bars, bakeries and meat markets, schools, shipbuilding, and masonry all came into being.

Life seemed mostly good and stable, bar the wrath of the elements. Like many islands in the Caribbean, St. Barths was subject to tropical storms and hurricanes, several of which hit the island, causing devastation and disease, and killing hundreds of people. If it wasn't rain wreaking havoc, it was drought, made all the worse because St. Barths is water deprived to begin with. Add to all that a monumental fire in 1852.

Still, the marriage between Sweden and St. Barths lasted ninety-four years. Increasingly, however, the island became a financial burden, and as early as 1868 Sweden tried to give it back to France as part of the dependency of Guadeloupe or find another interested party (including the United States . . . imagine!). In 1878, the Swedes were only too happy to return the irritating little pebble in the Caribbean to France as a dependent of Guadeloupe. It remained thus until 2009, when it gained autonomy from Guadeloupe. It is now its own collective and, as such, reports directly to the Ministry of Overseas in Paris.

Opposite: A colored engraving of eighteenth-century female pirate Anne Bonny, who sailed with Calico Jack Rackham throughout the Caribbean.

"*David Rockefeller brought his friends: Kissinger, Onassis, Edmond de Rothschild. That's when the spotlight started to shine on St. Barths. It became a rich guy's island—moreover, an old rich guy's island. Land values rose. Local people started selling their properties, which enabled them to send their kids to school off the island.*"

RANDY GURLEY
RESTAURATEUR

"*Jane and I bought Eden Rock in 1995. We were guests on a boat and we first saw it in the late afternoon. It, of course, made an impression. Then we came another time and stayed there. There were only six bedrooms. We originally were going to have it as our house. We were accidental hoteliers and ran Eden Rock like Fawlty Towers. I had never run a hotel before and was an unqualified nobody.*"

DAVID MATTHEWS
HOTELIER

Previous page: Gustavia watercolor on paper by Stanislas Defize.

The Reign Of Rémy

Between the nineteenth and mid-twentieth centuries, life on St. Barths passed quietly, without major incident. That changed with the coming of a French-Dutch adventurer. His name was Rémy de Haenen, and he can be credited with—or blamed for—what St. Barths has become, starting with his 1945 landing of his two-seater Rearwin Sportster in the grasslands of St. Jean, where the airport is now. By doing so, he introduced aviation to an island that was previously accessible only by boat.

He was also St. Barths's most passionate champion of progress; its most famous civil servant; the man who introduced clean water and electricity; the owner of Eden Rock (both his home and an inn); and a relentless womanizer. Stories abound. Myron Clement, whose public relations agency handled St. Barths, remembers his own first time on the island: "There was only one hotel—the Eden Rock. It had only six rooms, and its owner, Rémy de Haenen, was also the mayor of St. Barths, as well as a pilot who delivered mail back and forth from St. Martin, Statia [St. Eustatius], and Antigua to St. Barths." In other words, he was a one-man band.

Above, from left to right: Rémy de Haenen on Tintamarre Island, 1949; Haenen's first landing on nearby Saba, 1959; a view of the Eden Rock Hotel, Haenen's home-cum-inn, 1955.

David Matthews, the present owner of Eden Rock, remembers Haenen as a maverick. "He flew his plane with no shoes; none of his daughters wore shoes either. He helped women on the island who had difficult pregnancies to go to another island to have their babies. He had famously wild social skills but, still and all, was a catalyst for St. Barths. Haenen regarded the island as his fiefdom. He also drew people like Greta Garbo, Howard Hughes, and Robert Mitchum. He was a much loved man."

Not everyone holds Haenen in such esteem: "He was a pain in the ass," says one detractor, "and surrounded himself with beautiful women, including his two daughters." Myron's business partner, Joe Petrocik, knew one of them: "When we got to the Eden Rock, I met Hélène, who worked at the bar. She said to me, 'I hear you like Martinis.' I said, 'You don't look old enough to make one.'" She wasn't, but she did. "She proceeded to mix one, then another, and was becoming more beautiful as the sun was going down. She broke the spell when she suddenly said, 'You can make your own Martinis from now on. I have a date in Gustavia.'"

Geneviève Jouany, who ran Les Castelets until it was wiped away by Hurricane Luis in 1995, became friendly with Haenen and his wife, Giselle, when Geneviève and her husband came to live on the island part-time. "We rented a little *case*—essentially a room with a bed. I would come

every weekend from St. Thomas, where I was manager of a chain of gift shops. Rémy was then St. Barths' mayor. He would go to Puerto Rico to get food and supplies. He was commuting all the time. On Fridays, he would land on St. Thomas and pick me up. The landing strip on St. Barths was dirt, and there were sheep on it." Today the only things in flocks on the well-paved runway are private planes, and lots of them.

Haenen moved to Santo Domingo after he sold Eden Rock, but returned to St. Barths, where he died in 2008 at the age of ninety-two.

Native Son

Bruno Magras, president of St. Barths since 2009, recalls what it was like more than half a century ago. "I was born in Flamands in my mother's bedroom in a nice little wooden house close to the beach. Electricity came to the island in 1962, but we didn't have any until 1966. Until then my mother had to 'save' [preserve] the meat and fish with salt. The roads back then were poor. There was no potable water. It was a terrible situation. I left in 1967 because there was no work for me here. Many of us used to sail away to other islands. I went to St. Thomas and then joined the French army."

One of the first Americans to build on St. Barths was David Rockefeller. According to Magras, "when he came in 1975 to build his house in Colombier, he gave work to my people. By this time we were building roads and telephone fiber was put underground."

Magras has been involved in island politics for almost thirty years. But his emotional ties go back even further. "My father and grandfather were born here," he says. "The family name Magras comes from McGrath; we are from Ireland on my father's side. My mother's side was from France.

"The more I travel, the more I love my island. It is a safe place, which is not easy to maintain, because we are also an open island. There is the temptation of drugs, among other things. Social stability is an important factor in keeping the island secure. There is nothing worse than when some people get rich and others get poorer and poorer.

"We could have made many mistakes here," he continues, "because we were under pressure from developers. But we've fought hard to keep the island the way it is. There could have been a lot of concrete where there are still beautiful beaches. We have to be careful to keep up the economy, but not to destroy what is valuable in the process. We are now working on a zoning map with some hard rules. When I came back to St. Barths in 1971, one of my worries was keeping it from being developed, like St. Thomas—which is exactly what we don't want St. Barths to be."

Previous pages: La Vie Tranquille *watercolor on paper by Stanislas Defize; weaving a panama hat, 1959.*
Opposite: Bruno Magras, the president of St. Barths, was born in Flamands.

Les Femmes Mystiques

It is the women who were running the place. Socially and financially, they held the island together.
Jeet Singh, entrepreneur and musician

There are certain places where it seems as if you don't belong unless you possess the right physical attributes. In Aspen it means having a taut, muscular body resulting from rigorous downhill skiing in winter and hiking in the mountains in summer. On Capri, on the other hand, the bodies are more brazenly voluptuous and lubriciously bronzed (think Sophia Loren).

St. Barths is one of those places and is known especially for its beautiful women (OK, the men aren't bad either). Like the fabled girl from Ipanema, they carry themselves with poise and exude sex appeal. They are slim-hipped, ripe-breasted, and well suited, so to speak, to monokinis. Mostly they come from someplace else—usually France. But along with beauty, there are also those blessed with an entrepreneurial spirit. Several could even make a case for the superiority of women (at least on the island of St. Barths). And no one can doubt their determination.

Entrepreneurship started with some of the earliest Europeans to arrive on the island. The women of the community of Corossol, for example, descended from Norman, Breton, and Poitevin ancestors and have stubbornly carried on age-old traditions, like weaving straw to make hats and baskets, for centuries. To this day you can see them covered up in their printed cotton dresses, their skin weatherworn from the sun, and for special occasions wearing the traditional white cotton bonnet called a *calèche* or, alternatively, a *quichenotte* (which means "kiss me not"). While their husbands may have left to find work on other islands, they ruled the roost (and the roosters).

Geneviève Jouany's roost was a small luxury hotel called Les Castelets, which she managed until 1995. Petite but formidable, Geneviève is originally from La Rochelle in France. She and her husband crossed the Atlantic in a thirty-nine-foot sailboat in the early 1960s and eventually settled on St. Barths. Under Geneviève's supervision Les Castelets became a favorite hotel among dancers like Mikhail Baryshnikov from the American Ballet Theatre and Rudolf Nureyev. Other famous people followed. Now in her eighties, a widow, and living in a lovely home in Lorient, she has no regrets: "Things have changed a lot, but I still love it here."

Previous pages: Yachts (mega and otherwise) anchored in the picturesque harbor in Gustavia.
Opposite: St. Barths is known, among other things, for its exotically beautiful women.

So does Nicole Peraud, a filmmaker and documentarian who has been living on St. Barths on and off since the 1970s. She rents a house in Lorient. "My only regret is not having bought years ago. When I first came here"—her family is from Guadeloupe and Martinique—"there were only a few old Americans and the St. Bartians. The expats were funny and extravagant. Meanwhile, the St. Bartians were not at all shocked by the sight of half-naked people on their beaches.

"Life was cheap because there was nothing to buy," she says. "Today life here is more comfortable—you can rent a movie, find Parmesan cheese—but there are far too many cars on the island. Someone tried to introduce shuttle buses, but the taxi drivers drove him out. Years ago we walked a lot. We had more time. Today the Russians want to buy the whole island, but some things have no price. St. Barths is still a beautiful little laid-back island where you can live barefoot. Very small, but with a big spirit." Geneviève Jouany agrees: "The change doesn't bother me. The island is richer in all respects."

Richer, too, for its women.

The Queen Of Cuisine

While St. Barths has many excellent restaurants—which is one of its appeals—the most popular and most beloved is owned by a woman who is also the chef. Maya Gurley

Opposite: Catherine ("Cat") Cent, the Brigitte Bardot of St. Barths.

was born on Martinique and grew up on Guadeloupe (Nicole Peraud is her cousin). As a cook, she is self-taught. "My grandfather and father were making rum on Guadeloupe. I learned to make the spicy Creole salad on Maya's menu from the Creole cooks on the plantation."

Randy Gurley, Maya's American husband, met and married his wife when he was chartering his sailboat in the Caribbean. "Maya got pregnant in 1983," he says. "Our son, Nicolas, was born in January in France. We lived on board the boat with the baby. It became clear that babies and boats don't get along well. In the summer of 1984, we opened the restaurant with a partner. Maya has an incredible palate. She came from a family for whom food is vitally important. There were five brothers, lots of cousins, and many women—all of whom were competitive about cooking.

"Where Maya's is now," Randy says, "was a restaurant that didn't work. It was a shack called Chez Jackie and was all picnic tables, benches, and neon lights." By then the baby was a year old and Maya was pregnant again. She went to Martinique to have the second baby, another son. "I gave up my day job as a yacht charterer," he continues. "We bought out our partner that first summer and opened for dinner only. We hand wrote the menus every day and had about thirty people every night. I'd go into St. Martin to buy food.

"As Maya's took off, we became better at what we were doing. A stocky little French purveyor named Gerard Fior started a company called Foodland and worked closely with Maya. Until then, the only vegetable you could find on St. Barths was cabbage, because it lasted so long. But there were *boulangeries* selling fresh warm baguettes.

"Neither Maya nor I ever trained in the business," Randy says. "Her food was great. We had kids working for us who had wandering spirits and real personalities. The paved roads were minimal, and the cars mostly Mini Mokes and VWs. The dirt roads were so narrow that you'd have to pull over if you saw another car coming. There were only two hundred phones on the entire island; you had to wait for someone to die before you could get one."

In 2011, Maya's will have been in business for twenty-seven years, but it has the same simplicity as when it opened. "My idea for Maya's was to make people feel as if they were eating at home," Maya says. "We changed the seating and the deck, but the tin roof is the same. There's been a certain evolution regarding the food—more produce, for example. Some dishes are Creole, some are Thai; when I was living in Paris I used to go to Thai restaurants. The concept for the menu is more or less the same: a simple salad, a soup, a seviche or tartare, a main course, and a dessert. Everything is fresh. We serve a lot of local fish. Years ago the fishermen didn't catch mahimahi, only yellowtail snapper. We also used to have problems with poisonous fish and coral."

The location of Maya's, on the water and overlooking Gustavia, is unquestionably part of its draw ("At Christmas and New Year's, everything in Gustavia is lit and looks beautiful and

Opposite: Chef Maya Gurley in front of her popular, eponymous restaurant.

festive," Maya says). But so are its patrons. There's always somebody to see, like David Letterman ("He comes early, eats quickly, and doesn't linger"). There used to be a lot of fashion and film people, and in high season there still are; lately it attracts a lot of families. "I think we have the best clientele in the world," Maya says proudly.

A Breeder Of Boutiques

For such a small island, St. Barths has more than its share of shops proffering pareos, caftans, and teensy bikinis—the basics that no fashion-minded girl can be without in such a tropical clime. Designer labels like Hermès and Ralph Lauren abound too, but the brand that is most closely associated with St. Barths by those off the island is Calypso. The name comes variously from the sea nymph who held Odysseus captive, a kind of orchid, and music of the island of Trinidad. The store's original founder, Christiane Celle, opened the first Calypso in the Carré d'Or shopping area in Gustavia in 1992, and it was an immediate success. While Christiane later sold the brand in 2008 (there are now twenty-seven stores in twelve locations), her own connection with St. Barths continues because of her new boutique, Christiane Celle; Clic, her photo gallery in Gustavia; and the home she shares with her husband, the photographer Antoine Verglas, whom she met there. "I grew up in Cannes," Christiane says. "When I was in high school, my best friend, Pascal, moved to St. Barths on his own; he was one of the first. I'd always heard about the beauty of the island, but was never tempted to go, because it was known for windsurfing—one of the reasons Pascal went there. I thought it was too sporty for me. Finally I went to see Pascal. Because the island was perceived as being therapeutic, many young French boys and girls were being sent by their families to get [them] away from drugs.

"There were few hotels, only Eden Rock and one or two others. People would come with their own sheets and pillows. A lot of women gave birth at home because there was no hospital. As for restaurants, [Le] Tamarin had the only decent food on the island then. You could at least get a simple tomato and mozzarella salad, sometimes fresh fish. Cat [the owner] had macaws and was always going barefoot. She was like the Brigitte Bardot of St. Barths."

Christiane's attachment was both instantaneous and lasting. "On the day I was going home on my initial trip, I remember crying at the idea of leaving the island." She was among the first of many.

Opposite, clockwise from top left: Tropical gelato is the perfect treat after a day on the beach; the Calypso store on Gustavia's main street; signposts to nearby boutiques and specialty stores.

← CENTRE VILLE
SORTIE DE GUSTAVIA

↑ DIAMOND GENESIS

↑ CHANEL WATCHES

↑ ✦ PATEK PHILIPPE

↑ LIGNE ST BARTH
BOUTIQUE & SPA APPOINTMENT

↑ KOKON

VICTOIRE PRÊT A PORTER FEMME HOMME

↓ *Cartier*
50 m

↓ MARINE STORE
"*Le Ship*" - Tél: 05 90 27 86 29
www.ship-sb.com

↑ Restaurant 0590 27 31 67
LE VIETNAM vietnamiennes, chinos et thailandaises

↑ BONITO BAR · RESTAURANT

↑ MC 2° PIPIRI
SAINT BARTH BOUTIQUE

↑ THE HOUSE

← BVLGARI

La Belle Hélène

Hélène Muntal and her partner, Franck Garcia, were living primarily in Paris, sometimes in Verbier, and occasionally in Italy when the idea of St. Barths occurred to them in 1988. They had created something they called the "Cure," a combination of massage and nutrition that uses organic topical products they invented. They would spend a week with one to two clients at a time, to the point where their Cure became like a club. But they were traveling too much, feeling overly peripatetic. "We'd always wanted one place to settle in," Hélène says. They'd gone to Bermuda, but there were not enough waves for Franck, who is a surfer. They also often went to Guadeloupe, and although they'd heard about St. Barths, they were warned off it—told not to go because it was a "white" island and very snobbish.

One of their clients was Dena Kaye, a travel writer and the daughter of the American entertainer Danny Kaye. "Dena is the one who suggested doing the Cure in St. Barths," Hélène says. "Franck and I took a small plane. Next to me was this very elegant lady dressed in beige with a big Vuitton bag. 'Uh-oh, this is not going to be a place for me,' I said to myself. But the woman turned out to be very kind and kept explaining what was on the right and what was on the left of the plane. She was so sweet. I thought, 'Why am I thinking this way?' When we landed, one of the first things I saw was a surfer. I said excitedly, 'Look, Franck, there are waves here!'

"Here on this small island, I began to make custom-made products, mostly natural oils, tailored to our clients. My nickname as a child was Bébé Lou, so we called the products Belou. Everything is made in St. Barths using traditional methods, and all with a certification for organic products.

"It has been a true love story between St. Barths and us, even though what we had in mind for ourselves was the opposite of what it is. When we arrived here, we knew nothing about tax advantages. We didn't care. All we knew was that we felt immediately welcome. We did the Cure for Dena, and she asked us to stay for six more days. When we were on the plane returning to Paris, I began to cry. We came back the next year for good."

Pages 44–45: Le Select is rumored to serve the best burger on the island; Jeeps, cars, and motorbikes have replaced Mini Mokes when it comes to riding around St. Barths. *Previous pages:* An aerial view of the Eden Rock hotel on Baie de St. Jean. *Opposite:* Hélène Muntal.

The Wrath Of Luis

St. Barths, like other Caribbean and Atlantic islands, has a history of tempestuous storms. The warm-water corridor in which it's located, stretching from Africa to Central America, is known as Hurricane Alley. Come September through the end of October (although technically hurricane season runs from July to November), St. Bartians brace themselves or else leave altogether. Having been through hurricanes all too many times, they do not take them lightly. Hurricane Luis, which occurred in 1995, was one of the worst and most memorable.

Jane and David Matthews purchased Eden Rock from Rémy de Haenen in 1995. Coming from their home in England with their youngest son, Spencer, they were just in time to be greeted by Luis. Here is David's account:

"We had arrived in St. Barths three days before, looking for a new and more adventurous life . . . . The beautiful but badly run-down house and buildings . . . yielded not much in the way of anti-hurricane barricades or equipment. But the house was built of stone and hardwood and looked strong enough [to stay there] . . . .

Above: A satellite image of Hurricane Luis, 1995.

"Rapidly the wind increased until it screamed through every weak joint in our defenses and tugged and yanked mightily at the coconut trees and island buildings . . . . We prayed we would survive this thing together.

"We looked outside and watched a phenomenon develop. Within an hour, the sky and sea had disappeared. Their space became one gray mass of smashing, hammering wind and water that was not so much blowing as delivering incessant tearing concussions that staggered the air, sea, buildings, seemingly the very land itself and everything that stood attached to it . . . .

"After about forty hours, Luis drifted north . . . .

"Back on St. Barths, people emerged and began to look around. Houses and hotels had been flung into the sea. Water and electricity plants were so badly damaged as to remain out of service for the following three weeks . . . .

"Tragically . . . there were human fatalities, as well as thousands of animals large and small— so many, in fact, as to poison the sea. (Swimming was banned for three weeks.)"

Had the Matthewses believed in omens, they might have turned around and beaten a hasty retreat back to England. Instead, they stayed.

On The Beaches

On our first trip, we had a shack on the beach at Les Mouettes. One day my daughter Alex found a hairless dog full of fleas, but with a great face. She followed us everywhere and we all fell in love with her.
Sylvie Chantecaille, cosmetics
and fragrance entrepreneur

You can find beautiful beaches all over the world, from the coast of California to the South Pacific, and there are many in the Caribbean that rival St. Barths in their expanse, the texture of their sand, their privacy, their aquatic creatures, and the clarity and colors of their waters. But for a St. Barths aficionado, nothing compares to bobbing around like a buoy in the island's salt water—temperature consistently around eighty degrees—wearing next to nothing or indeed nothing at all.

There are anywhere from fourteen to twenty-two beaches to choose from, depending on the guide or map you consult. Some are more accessible than others, some more rugged, but all have their special features. Lorient is a favorite of local families and windsurfers; Grand Cul de Sac is lined with

Previous pages: Sunset on Shell Beach in Gustavia
is a good time to find treasures from the sea.

Sisters Alex Chantecaille and Olivia Chantecaille.

Pointe
Petit Jean

Baie de
St. Jean

Colombier

Corossol

Gustavia

Grande Pointe

Point Lorient

Lorient

Grand-Cul de-Sac

Petit-Cul de-Sac

Saint Jean

Pages 56–57: A satellite image of St. Barths. The island has been called "a dollop of France dropped into the Caribbean";
Previous pages: These tropical waters may look placid but they're also great for catching waves.

rustic restaurants, boat rentals, and shacks; on Shell Beach there are . . . you guessed it; Grand Fond is for collectors of sea glass (see box on page 75), shells, and coral. Herewith la crème de la crème:

St. Jean: This is where Rémy de Haenen landed his plane in the late 1940s and where the airport is located. That means that anyone having a swim in the *baie* can witness the small planes arriving and taking off. Noisy it can be, but being based here at one of the hotels or cottages is akin to attending a daily air show and is especially captivating for kids. While not exceptionally wide, the crescent-shaped beach at St. Jean has fine-grained sand and plenty of activity, especially in high season. Tropical storms have taken their toll, however, and erosion is the result.

Colombier: This beach, in the northwest of the island, is as difficult to reach as St. Jean is easy. Known for being where David Rockefeller built his house, which still stands, it is accessed either by boat (and is a preferred spot to anchor and overnight), seaplane, or helicopter—or on foot. It is also said to have more rocks and islets than any other place on the island. Sea turtles and bird life abound. And if you want to fish, this is one of the best areas. Getting to it on foot means wending your way through what used to be a donkey path, lately widened, lined with tall and spiky torch cacti. It takes a good thirty to forty minutes to get there, but it's worth it.

Above: The crescent shaped St. Jean beach offers views of small planes taking off or landing on the nearby runway.

Flamands: If you stay at the Hôtel Saint-Barth Isle de France, you will be cozily ensconced in this lovely, peaceful *anse* (cove). If there is such a thing as extra-fine-grain sand, Flamands has it aplenty. And you needn't be a hotel guest to enjoy the beach. All St. Barths' beaches are public, even if some seem more private than others.

Saline: Unlike on Flamands, there are no hotels (at least not yet, and, one hopes, never) on this wonderful stretch, close to the old salt-harvesting operations. *Salin* literally means "salt marsh." The marsh isn't the prettiest sight on the island, and because no work goes on here any longer, it feels lonely—except for the birds—and a little eerie. The payoff is *la plage*. It's a small hike to get there, but it is splendid. Not many bathers wear swimsuits, so be prepared for flashes of flesh.

Gouverneur: Situated on the southern coast, this beach, like Saline, is great for early-morning and late-afternoon walks. The road to Gouverneur is long and winding, the beach barely visible until you actually set foot on it, which is an experience in itself, for the sand has been compared to baby powder, sifted flour, and even cashmere. The cliffs protect it, giving it a sense of isolation, as if it were just you and the mountain goats that romp along the hillside. Swimming there is one of the island's most sensual and salubrious treats.

Colombier

"That's what I like about St. Barths. It's very small—but there are so many places here you can be on the island and not see someone you know for a week."

PATRICK DEMARCHELIER,
PHOTOGRAPHER

Opposite: The entry to Saline beach.

Rose Marie Bravo and Bill Jackey toast the good life.

Jean Pagliuso, 1977.

Kelly Bensimon.

A hand-woven Panama hat is a must-have souvenir. Opposite: A bikini and a pareo are (almost) all one needs to pack.

Left: St. Barths's aquamarine water. Right: Calypso founder Christiane Celle.

Gouverneur

Kite surfing is another popular watersport.

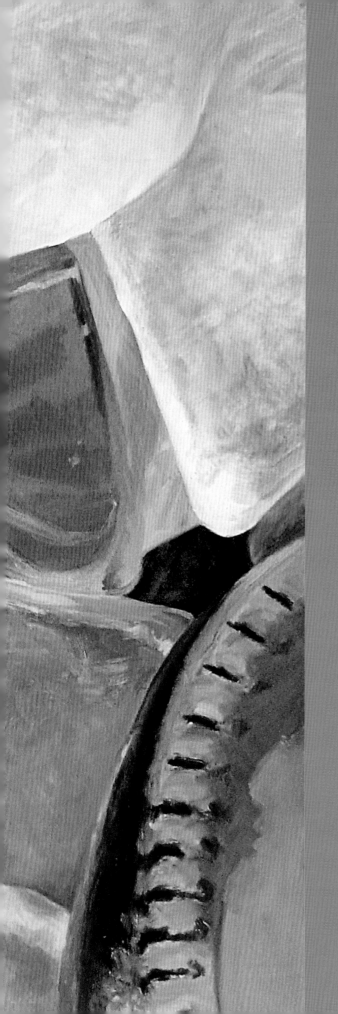

Gifts From The Sea

Some beach lovers collect shells of all shapes and sizes and bring them home as souvenirs. Retailer Rose Marie Bravo and her husband, William (Bill) Jackey, are far more passionate about what Bill calls "other people's garbage." He means sea glass, those relics that come from shipwrecks or from more ordinary places, such as discarded bottles, tableware, and other household items. Often this colorful detritus is washed up on the beach or in the surf. At its prettiest, it has a frosty surface from years of erosion and hydration and comes in colors as varied as turquoise, purple, cobalt blue, yellow, red, orange, and even black. Much of it is junk, but for connoisseurs, sea glass is as precious as pearls.

"We go to Grand Fond or Lorient," says Rose Marie, the former CEO of Burberry. "It all began one year when we rented another place on St. Barths because the one we wanted wasn't available. It was right on the beach. In the house was a bowl of this colored glass. I asked the maid what it was, and she told me we could find it on our very beach. That's how it started. It's become a hobby for both of us.

"We cover ourselves up and spend hours in the water looking for the best of it. We put what we find in buckets, take it home, and then go over what we've found. I'm the gatherer; Bill is the editor. It's something we can do together and is great fun not only for us, but for our grandchildren."

Previous pages: A surf shop on Lorient; on the beach at Eden Rock. *Opposite:* An oil-on-canvas painting of the seaglass found on Grand Fond and Lorient.

Actress Susan Forristal heading out for a swim, 1983.

Opposite: Sea turtles abound in the waters off Colombier.
This page: The sand in St. Barths has been compared to cashmere.

An Island Transformed

Things really changed when for a short period the cruise liners came into Gustavia.
To escape, we would go to Corossol, this community that spoke their own native Creole patois.
The women all wore these little dresses. You couldn't tell if they were twenty-one or eighty-one.
They were all thin, their skin ravaged by the sun.
Jean Pagliuso, photographer

By the second half of the twentieth century, St. Barths was ready, but for what wasn't quite clear. Rémy de Haenen, now mayor of St. Barths, had installed electricity, telephone lines, and water. Small airlines, like Winair, were providing semi-regular service. David Rockefeller finished building his modern house in Colombier and introduced his wealthy and worldly friends to the island, among them the French financier Edmond de Rothschild, who bought a large piece of property in Marigot, in the eastern part of St. Barths. Along with Rothschild came his family, his coterie, and his mistress (in a separate house, *bien sûr*). Others followed. But the island was still difficult to get to and offered far too few amenities to appeal to average tourists. All to the good, some would say.

While it may not have been an ideal place for a vacation—yet—it was still a beautiful place to photograph. "The reason this tiny island became the St. Barths of today," Joe Petrocik contends, "was because of the fashion business. Photographers like Bill Connors, who shot many covers for *Glamour* in the late 1960s, used St. Barths as a backdrop for fashion shoots. After Connors came Patrick Demarchelier. Then there were all those Slim Aarons portfolios in *Town & Country*." The exposure St. Barths received from those stories raised people's awareness of it, as well as piqued the curiosity of seasoned travelers looking for the next place.

"Yes, it was the photographers who put it on the map," remembers Antoine Verglas, who came to St. Barths in the late 1980s and early 1990s. By then, he remembers, "It was becoming like South Beach."

Not only did Antoine shoot on the island, he found his wife there: "I was working for Elite models, Victoria's Secret, French *Elle*, and others. Christiane [Celle] and I met in 1993 at Eddy's Ghetto, which was owned by the son of Marius Stakelborough of Le Select. Our first son, Julian, was raised on St. Barths. He's now a surfer and kite surfer, no doubt because of where he grew up."

Opposite: Photographers fell in love with St. Barths, ultimately putting it on the map with their seductive images.

St. Barths may be synonymous with Caribbean chic, but it's equally great for a family vacation.

Eden Rock Hotel owners, David and Jane Matthews, with their sons James and Spencer.

Roman Abramovich and Cindy Crawford.

Calvin Klein and Jann Wenner.

A motorbike is another way to get around, but thanks to the uneven streets, they're not for the faint-hearted. Below: Griffin Dunne and Lorraine Kirke, 2001.

Princess Diana on vacation in St. Barths, 1995.

Antoine felt a change in the place in 1995, three years after Christiane had opened Calypso. "That's when people like Peter Brant and DeNiro started coming. Puff Daddy [as Sean Combs was then known] began giving his parties at Nikki Beach in 1999 or 2000. The island became crazy at places like Autour du Rocher; today [David] Letterman owns that land. Le Banane was the most interesting cabaret. You didn't feel the wealth back then, but it was definitely and surreptitiously there.

"St. Barths gives a very elegant style to the Caribbean," Antoine continues, "but it is not fancy. There is no artifice—you could get naked on the beach—but it is exclusive. It is always glamorous, but in a natural way."

Being a French island, St. Barths holds good food in high esteem. Gradually, restaurants opened, dedicating themselves to creating dishes that no place else in the Caribbean was serving. Restaurateurs began importing ingredients and bringing in from France not only wines, but chefs and sommeliers. Eventually, hotels like Eden Rock, Les Castelets, François Plantation, and Le Toiny became known as much for their restaurants as for their accommodations. This significantly raised the bar on St. Barths, and the island began attracting food writers, like Lee Bailey and the *New York Times* restaurant critic Craig Claiborne.

Ruth Schwartz, who used to do public relations for Bloomingdale's, recalls how Craig brought St. Barths to her attention: "I used to run morning breakfast programs at our stores. Craig would come in and talk about this new small appliance called the Cuisinart. One day I picked him up and drove him to our store in Short Hills [New Jersey]. He looked tan and unusually relaxed. I asked him where he'd been, and he said, 'I'll tell you later, but you can't tell anyone else.'" Those who frequented St. Barths were like a secret society.

Retired executive Bruce Gordon echoes this sentiment: "You made a pact that you wouldn't tell anyone about St. Barths. Those of us who loved it lived in fear that it would find its way onto the radar."

Ruth not only went to the island in 1975 (and, like Craig, stayed at the Hotel Le Village St. Jean), she still goes and now has an even more special connection. "My daughter I. B. was a dancer. One time she went on vacation there. I told her that if she ever went, she would never come back." Sure enough, I. B. fell in love with a young Frenchman. His mother is Gaby Charneau, who owns the Hotel Le Village St. Jean. Now married twenty-three years, I. B. and Bertrand Charneau run a popular restaurant, deli and catering place across from Nikki Beach called Kiki-é Mo. As for Craig Claiborne, he went every Christmas for years until he became ill. He felt so at home that he kept an extra set of pots and pans and his trusty Cuisinart at the hotel. "He always stayed in Villa No. 10 and made wonderful meals there," I. B. says. "On one trip, he actually came into the kitchen and cooked with the staff. He had a great time."

Pages 82–83: Gustavia harbor lit up at dusk. *Pages 84–85:* Calvin Klein, Jean Pagliuso, Nona Summers, Diane von Furstenberg, and Susan Forristal. *Opposite:* John Loeffler and Tom Cohen on St. Jean, 1984.

" We love the beautiful beaches. I learned to swim in St. Barths. There's such a variety from calm, nearly placid, to deep, beautiful waves. The restaurants are wonderful and plentiful —something for all palates. I also love the obvious, casual chic of the island and the ease of getting around. "

ALICIA BYTHEWOOD
PHILANTHROPIST

" I became friends with Lorne Michaels, who brought in the right people—funny, smart, and interesting people. Immediately, the island caught on. He kept bringing in performing artists. That was twenty years ago. "

KINO BACHELLIER
DOCTOR

Previous pages: A sunset swim with wraparound views, *bien sûr.*

" St. Barths is my annual mecca and an important part of balancing my life. The thought of it changing is a terrible one because there is no place like it in the Caribbean. "

BRUCE GORDON
RETIRED CORPORATE EXECUTIVE

" Last year, we stayed for four weeks in January and February and loved it. The warm breezes, the fresh bread, the wines, the local people. All we took were two duffel bags. Mine was packed with caftans, swimsuits and pareos. You don't need anything else. "

ROSE MARIE BRAVO
RETAILER

Previous pages: Ralph Gibson on the airstrip, 1977. *Above:* The pool at Eden Rock's Villa Rockstar.

Another food writer, Anthony Bourdain, takes a much dimmer view of St. Barths In his second memoir, *Medium Raw*, in a chapter called "The Rich Eat Differently than You and Me" he lashes into the island: "I knew that St. Barths . . . was not somewhere I could ever be happy. I knew from previous day trips that a hamburger and a beer cost fifty bucks—that there was no indigenous culture to speak of, that it was the very height of the holiday season and the island, not my scene in the best of circumstances, would be choked with every high-profile douche, Euro-douche, wannabe, and oligarch with a mega-yacht. I knew enough of the place to know that St. Barths was not for me." He is speaking of the St. Barths of now, not of yore.

Others, even those who love the island, concur that the Christmas holidays are exactly the time to avoid St. Barths. As festive as Gustavia may look when all lit up like a Christmas tree, it is almost impossible to drive through, thanks to traffic jams created by merrymakers, much less get a parking space. And just try getting a table at Maya's. The harbor is as jammed as the streets, and everyone looks familiar, particularly if you are a New Yorker. And if you are not a New Yorker and don't especially like New Yorkers to begin with, you'd best go elsewhere (not that you could get a hotel reservation anyway).

Above: Tammy Bruno and Jean Pagliuso, 1989.

But one person's nightmare is someone else's dream, so there are those who couldn't imagine being any place else for New Year's. It is party time, all day and all night. The restaurants are packed, the villas rented, the clubs and bars abuzz with fun-loving, fashionable types. Even the mega-yachts anchored off the beach at Colombier seem to be swaying to the music.

The list of regulars at holiday time and high season over recent years reads like a "Page Six" anthology: Ronald Perelman and Paul Allen (on their mega-yachts), Sean Combs, Russell Simmons, Naomi Campbell, Ivanka Trump, the Hilton sisters, the Qaddafi brothers, Anna Wintour, David Letterman, Steve Martin, Jimmy Buffett, and Lorne Michaels. As it is with many resorts, where the leader of the pack goes, others follow, until they form a tight little like-minded community who eat together, play together, and live in each other's back pockets for the duration of their stay.

Jimmy Buffett, of course, wrote the hit song "Cheeseburger in Paradise." While he may not have had the burger at Le Select—the most popular hangout in Gustavia—in mind, he nonetheless paid homage to the bar's owner, Marius Stakelborough. Jimmy and his band gave a free concert at Le Select for the bar's sixtieth anniversary.

" Nureyev, the dancer of the century, lived here for many years in a house that is now historical and legendary. He chose the place for its magic and it is magical, especially at sunset. And if you have the good fortune to be naked under a warm and windy rain shower then you know all your sins have been washed away. You love life and life loves you. "

JEANNE AUDY-ROWLAND
AUTHOR

Opposite: Part-time St. Bartian Jeanne Audy-Rowland bought the house built for Rudolf Nureyev. He called it his *dacha*.

Opposite page, top: Yachts at Gustavia harbor. *Opposite page, bottom:* A lazy day on the deck. *This page, clockwise from top left:* Jet Skis for hire in the port of Gustavia; Bill Jackey and friend; windsurfers; Ron Delsener, Lorne Michaels, John Head, and Samantha Delsener, 1978.

La Vie En Villa

We rent a villa at the top of St. Jean called Super Sky.
From there, we can see Lorient, Saline, and St. Martin at sunset.
Rose Marie Bravo, retailer and former CEO of Burberry

St. Barths has no shortage of excellent hotels—Eden Rock, Le Sereno, the Saint-Barth Isle de France, Le Guanahani, and Le Toiny, to name a few—and one could be sublimely happy for a few days while being gently administered to in luxurious, full-service surroundings. Many visitors, however, prefer to rent a villa. Owning one, of course, is even better, but you need the patience of Job to get it built or restored. St. Barths is a remote island, after all, and island time is slower and more methodical and, when it comes to getting things done, can become tangled in layers of bureaucracy. Aside from all this, real estate on St. Barths is wildly expensive, and not much of it is available. This didn't deter David Rockefeller from constructing his personal Arcadia in Colombier, and it hasn't discouraged Russian billionaire Roman Abramovich, who bought former dot-commer-cum-rock-musician Jeet Singh's multi-structure mega-villa on Gouverneur for a reported 65 million euros. But wait: There are bargains (relatively speaking) to be had. According to Christian Wattiau of Sibarth, the most prestigious firm specializing in rentals and sales, most houses are in the $3.4 million to $13.5 million range, and there are even a few for sale for a mere $2 million to $4 million.

Among the most popular Sibarth villas to rent is the one owned by Dena Kaye and her partner, architect Richard Fallin. It is modest in size and located in Pointe Milou, affording magnificent views and a guaranteed sunset on most nights. "We found the house after looking for a couple of seasons," Dick says, "and it was one that had the simplest of plans—living, dining, kitchen, two small bedrooms and baths, one small deck, one bathtub-sized pool, and a one-car garage. It was sited on a hillside in a nice way, but of the three sensational sea views, only one was used. The house had no real entry; you sort of wandered up the hill until you found the front door. We were fortunate to find a team of local professionals to help us realize our goals and who made everything, regardless of the horror stories we'd heard, go like clockwork."

So began the transformation of another couple's 1980s dream house: opening the walls to get the views; removing the tired floor tiles; reconfiguring the bedrooms and baths; redoing the kitchen

Opposite: Wide open vistas at the Sibarth-managed Villa WIK guarantee superb sunsets.

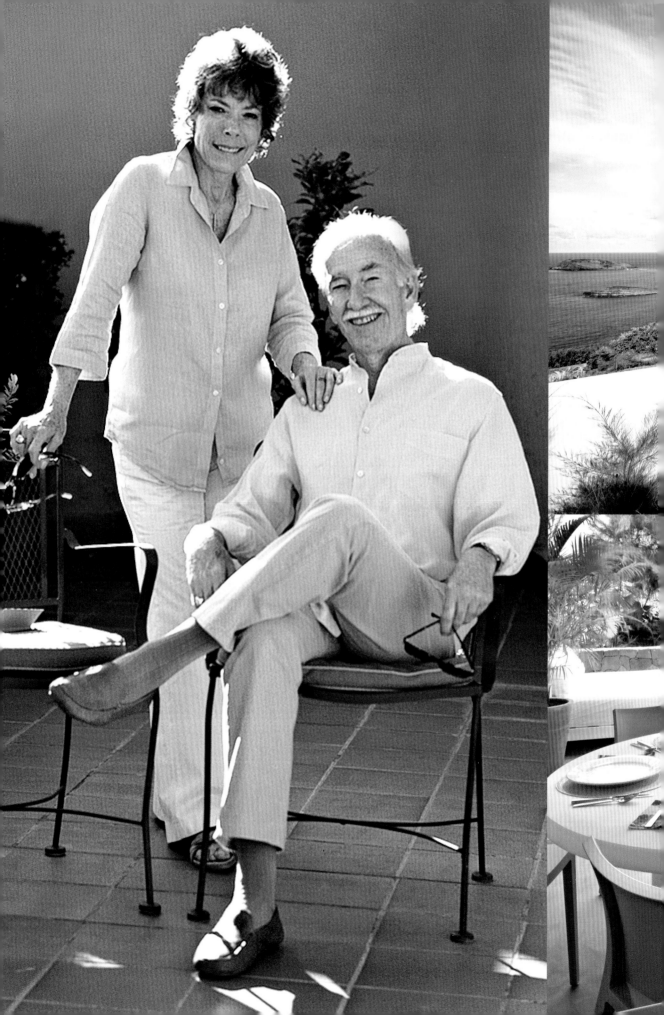

with sleek marine-grade stainless steel countertops; installing some real lighting; and carving out the side of the hill for a long lap pool and terrace. "For the interior, we decided that contrary to our last house [in Aspen], this one would be simple, simple, simple: I designed all the built-in furniture in a lightly stained ash wood, soft gray-white walls, light gray-green epoxy flooring, and light-gray-toned wood ceilings," Dick says. "It is a very soothing palette, and no clutter. It has become our winter refuge, a place to decompress."

Dick's significant other has been going to St. Barths since the early '80s: "I was on a cruise of the surrounding islands," Dena says, "and when we spent the day in St. Barths, I loved it so much, I just plain jumped ship." After renting for years, Dena was almost destined to one day be an owner. "When we thought about other islands where one would spend two to three months, St. Barths came out on top because of the variety of things to do. Walking every day on an empty beach for months with no other diversions wasn't a satisfying concept." Unless you're Robinson Crusoe.

Villa SIB DKD, as it is called, is one of the most popular houses in the Sibarth collection because of its size, its location, and the superb views—perfect for a couple and occasional guests. If its owners didn't have the audacity to stay there for several months at a time, it could be rented year-round.

Opposite: Dena Kaye and Richard Fallin. *This page, above and below:* Kaye and Fallin opened their home to the views and created a breakfast room.

Roger Lacour, who is originally from Guadeloupe, and his American wife, Brook, started Sibarth in 1975. The reason, he says, was simple. "Most everyone staying for a few days or more was asking me the same question: 'Is there a small piece of land to buy, because I would love to have a little *case* [small house] on the island?' I said to myself that if everyone succeeds in finding land, who is going to take care of their real estate when they are not on the island?" As land became more and more expensive—St. Barths is, after all, only eight square miles—the little *case* became bigger and bigger. Today, many homeowners choose to work with rental companies to let others enjoy their home when they aren't there.

Sibarth today both sells and rents properties to a sophisticated and demanding clientele. "Our people travel all over the world," Roger says. "When they come to St. Barths, they want to find what they have at home." And more. This means a well-designed, stylishly furnished house with a great view, a pool, a couple of deck chairs, a flat-screen TV, Internet access, the works. And they are willing to pay the price. If, for example, the house they've rented does not have American channels so they can watch the Super Bowl, they become nuts"—an emotional state that's hardly conducive to a relaxing vacation.

Pages 106–107: As the sun sets, the pool at Villa SIB DKD invites an evening dip. *Opposite:* The all-white theme of Villa WIK in the Sibath collection draws the eye to the splendor outside.

109

Previous pages: Los Leones, the home of Catherine and Pero Feric at Pointe Milou. *Clockwise from top:* Finding property to buy is not easy on St. Barths. Luckily this house was offered to photographer Patrick Demarchelier; the pool overlooks Gustavia, the western end of the island, and has views of the Caribbean beyond; Dermachelier's St. Barths hideaway; the living room has an eclectic mix of wicker and wood-and-cane furniture from Sri Lanka and Barbados; Dermarchelier with his Swedish wife, Mia, and their three sons (from left) Arthur, Victor, and Gustav.

> *I had a lemonade stand on Flamands Beach in front of the Taiwana hotel, where we always stayed. Someone gave my kids a twenty-dollar bill for a glass of lemonade. We gave all the donations to the church in town that night at dusk. Some memories you never want to forget.*

KELLY BENSIMON
MODEL AND ACTRESS

> *People on St. Barths who keep to themselves are called 'goats.'*

GRACE LEO
HOTELIER

"*We all lived in a house in Gustavia. We would start cooking at four in the afternoon and would end up with twenty people by the time we were ready to sit down.*"

NICOLE PERAUD
FILMMAKER

"*There is no metro system, no public transport, no cultural life here. It's just a little eight-square-mile island.*"

DAVID MATTHEWS
OWNER OF EDEN ROCK

Clockwise, from top left: Architects and interior designers Donato Savoie and Antonio Morello of Studio MORSA built the villa for Liz Claiborne and Art Ortenberg; the bedroom with wraparound glass walls; the oasis-like pool; the lounge is decorated to resemble an African lodge; the picturesque music room.

Previous pages: The kidney-shaped pool at the Sibarth-managed Villa JAY. *Clockwise from top:* The volcanic lava stone infinity-edged pool at Villa DOL in Point Milou; from the living room you can see the sunrise over Tortue and set over Lorient and St. Jean; a sleek bathroom; Villa DOL has a more poetic name too: Villa La Danse Des Etoiles (Dance of the Stars).

Celebration Isle

It was such a pleasure to see Olivia and Ren [Warren] relax and fall into island time. Their wedding ceremony was followed by dinner and dancing on the terrace of a private villa. A long table was strung up with chandeliers covered in fresh orchids. The only thing to outshine the stars was the surprise fireworks display that Ren arranged as a gift for his new bride.
Julie Skarratt, photographer

Much to the dismay of many St. Bartians, their home has gained a reputation as a 24/7 party island. While this is an exaggeration, there are certain times of the year that lend themselves to breaking out the Cristal, pumping up the volume, and dancing until dawn, such as any day between Christmas and New Year's and during the Bucket Regatta—the sailboat race, usually held in March, that is now one of the most prestigious in the world and one of the events that put St. Barths on the map for sailing aficionados. Often enough, people come to the island in groups, which is akin to bringing your own party. Their reportedly was one on pristine Gouverneur. "To those who consider that beach practically sacred ground, this signaled the end of St. Barths as they knew it," one shocked visitor says. (Perhaps the zoning map that President Magras promises will prevent such goings-on in the future.)

Less intrusive festivities are tolerated, and because St. Barths is physically so lovely, it provides a perfect setting for such sentimental occasions as birthdays, engagements, and anniversaries, not to mention romantic ones, like first and second honeymoons and, of course, weddings.

Ask those who know the islands of the Caribbean which is the most romantic and surely St. Barths will be high on the list, if not in first place. Supermodel Paulina Porizkova got married there, as did the now-divorced Russell Simmons and Kimora Lee (warning: St. Barths can guarantee a romantic wedding, but not a lifetime of wedded bliss).

When Gretchen and Dwight Fenton decided to get married on the island in 2003, Gretchen (née Gunlocke) was the fashion director for *Town & Country* magazine. They had their reasons: small wedding, small island. "I had been four or five times before," Gretchen says. "We were leaning toward St. Barths. Then I went on a shoot for *T&C*, which sealed our decision." The assignment, ironically, was to seek out the best looking men on the island for a photo portfolio, hardly an

Opposite: Olivia Chantecaille and her husband, Warren (Ren) Grady III, moments after their ceremony in Gustavia.

unpleasant task. "Both the men and the women on the island are very natural and carefree. They have honey-golden tans and amazing smiles." Nevertheless, Gretchen decided to bring her own good-looking man with her and ended up marrying him.

Their ceremony took place at St. Bartholomew's Anglican Church in Gustavia, in a service performed by the church's vicar, the Reverend Charles Vere Nicoll, who also owns the Hôtel Saint-Barth Isle de France, where the couple honeymooned. The vicar is particular about the ceremonies he officiates: "I do not want this island to become like Las Vegas, so I insist that the ceremony be performed in the church"—as opposed to on the beach, at poolside, or in a nightclub. But that didn't prevent a little partying at the Fentons' reception afterward: "The men were even taking their shirts off and jumping into the ocean," Gretchen says.

Olivia Chantecaille, whose family founded the high-end cosmetics and treatment company named for it, had her heart set on St. Barths, as did her fiancé, Warren (Ren) Grady III. "We chose it for several reasons," Olivia says. "We wanted a destination wedding so we could take people away from their everyday lives and have a wonderful time for several days. Also, St. Barths is French, and my family, also French, spent a lot of time there over the years. It would be fairly easy to get to for our relatives in France and also for our guests coming from the States." Choosing St. Barths turned out to be not only the biggest decision the couple made, but the right one as well. Once they had locked in the location, everything else fell into place. "I knew what kind of dress to wear," Olivia says, "what clothes to bring, more or less what the weather would be like and the kind of backdrop we had to work with—all those key elements. We also knew exactly what house we wanted for the reception, because my mother had seen it the summer before and showed it to us. It's in Carénage and has the most extraordinary views.

"We decided to be married in May because the weather would be good. We chose a weekend that didn't fall over a major holiday so our friends and family would be more inclined to come. After a long winter, they'd be dying for a taste of the tropics."

As far as the food went, they wanted to work with Maya. "Ren and I love her restaurant. Everything Maya makes is delicious. She also knows how to take care of everything—and everybody."

Randy Gurley, Maya's husband, suggested that Olivia and Ren meet local events planner Melanie Smith. But it was the last day of their scouting trip, and they had a plane to catch. They had just enough time to make a quick stop at Maya's To Go, the Gurleys' popular take-out place across from the airport. "When we're in St. Barths, we're at Maya's To Go every single day," Olivia says. "We were standing at the counter when Randy came running into the store and exclaimed, 'I was in my office, looked up at the screen, and saw that you were standing right next to Melanie.' That's how we met." Olivia gives high marks to Melanie: "She was amazing at being on top of everything on the day of the wedding and made sure that everyone did their jobs. It relieved me of having to worry about every other detail."

A barefoot bride and groom on a beach.

Above: Jimmy and Chandra Johnson's getaway car. Above, right: Final touches for an island bride. Left: An ocean-inspired place card.

Left: Gretchen and Dwight Fenton. Below: A candlelit table at the Johnson's Nikki Beach reception.

Above: Rose petals and romance.
Below: Olivia Chantecaille.

66 *We opened Maya's To Go in 2001, which was a success right away. We realized that many people don't want to go shopping for food or cook in their villas. Often, they don't want to go out at all. So we made it easy for them. Now we even make wedding cakes.* 99

MAYA GURLEY
RESTAURATEUR

66 *We started going thirty years ago with our children. We'd spend every Christmas vacation there for years. It was very comfortable and relaxed, the beaches weren't crowded. The restaurants were happy to have the kids. You could get a babysitter easily.* 99

ELLEN LEVINE
MAGAZINE EDITOR

"St. Barths defies economic cycles. It is always in style, always in fashion. Most often compared to St. Tropez, it also keeps reinventing itself and, because it is not a cheap destination, it will remain a playground for the rich and famous."

GRACE LEO
HOTELIER

"As nice as people on the island can be, they can also be peculiar. There used to be a woman in the bakery in Lorient. If she didn't like you, she would say, 'Sorry, no more bread,' just like that."

SYLVIE CHANTECAILLE
COSMETICS AND FRAGRANCE ENTREPRENEUR

Gretchen Fenton seconds that: "Melanie knows everyone on the island, from the florist to the minister at the church. She found a wonderful man to sing at the ceremony and hired steel-band players for the reception. Maya did the food and made our cake, which many said was the best wedding cake they'd ever had."

Olivia, who is a stickler when it comes to her appearance (would you expect anything less, considering the business she's in?), had her hair done by a local salon but brought someone down to do makeup from the firm's Miami branch because "I wanted a simple, natural look."

The only thing that wasn't natural was what happened to the groom the day before the wedding: "Ren loves to surf, so there he was in the waters of the beach at Le Toiny when he stepped between the coral onto a spiky sea urchin and injured both feet. He finally found a doctor who was open on Saturday morning to remove the needles, one by one." Ouch. A St. Barths version of cold feet?

Melanie Smith started organizing weddings and events fifteen years ago. As an American living on a French island and knowing it intimately, she was approached to assist with planning celebrations. Soon it became a business. She has since organized dozens of wedding parties, not only for Americans, but also for wealthy Europeans and South Americans, as well as for the St. Barths Bucket Regatta.

This page, above: A page boy does it island style in a tuxedo and shorts. *Below:* Olivia Chantecaille and Warren Grady III. *Opposite:* St. Bartholomew's Anglican Church.

Wedding Wisdom

Should you wish to get married on St. Barths,
here are a few things to keep in mind:

Make sure it's legal. Until recently, non-resident couples needed to secure their marriage license in their home country. But the laws on the island have changed. According to wedding planner Melanie Smith, a non-resident couple can now be legally married on the island as long as they have applied for the correct licenses six to eight months before the wedding. A wedding planner can help couples to do this.

Size matters. Because St. Barths is a small island, you are limited, perforce, to the number of guests you can have in a hotel or restaurant—usually no more than 100. Or you can rent a villa, but even then, few are large enough to accommodate a crowd.

Use locals for your food and planning. It's easier, more authentic, and more affordable. According to Gretchen Fenton, "We didn't want it to feel as if we'd brought New York to St. Barths. I sent a couple of things down that we couldn't find on the island, like hurricane lamps and place cards, but that was all."

Be flexible. You may not be able to find something you have your heart set on—a specific flower or a certain wine. Roll with it, or import it.

Be patient. "This is not the United States," Melanie cautions. "Obtaining proposals and quotes may not happen very quickly here. Life runs at a different pace and affects issues such as bidding jobs, putting together a proposal, etc. Also, there may not be three or four suppliers to recommend."

Remain optimistic. Melanie is confident that the talent pool on St. Barths "is astoundingly competent and professional."

Expect to pay for what you get—and vice versa. If you want a wedding on the cheap, St. Barths is the wrong choice.

Brace yourselves. "Everyone you invite will RSVP 'yes' to a wedding on St. Barths," Gretchen says. This may entail the couple (and their nearest and dearest) having to assume expanded roles as hosts-at-the-ready.

Opposite: The Fentons' tiered wedding cake, courtesy of Maya's, takes on a romantic glow in the candlelight.

Essential
St. Barths

"The first hotel where I stayed in 1979 was $32 a night. The water was solar heated. The food in the island's stores looked the way it does in Cuba—empty shelves, no lemons or limes."
Jean Pagliuso, photographer

St. Barths is one of the French West Indies (along with St. Martin, Martinique, and Guadeloupe). Its main language is French, although English is widely spoken. Getting there usually requires flying to St. Martin and then taking a small plane for the ten-minute-or-so flight into St. Barths. Another excellent option is Tradewind Aviation. If you don't fly commercial (on Winair or Air Caraïbes), you can charter a plane—that is, unless you own one. But the aircraft has to be small enough—usually a STOL (short take-off and landing). Warning: Prepare for a steep descent, which thrills some and unnerves others (see box on page 141). Alternatives: Take the ferry from St. Martin or hire a boat from there or another nearby island. You may encounter rough seas.

Bright island essentials, including embroidered beach totes, are available at Terra St. Barths in St. Jean.

St. Barths Style

As in St. Tropez, Capri, and other worldly resorts, the dress for women is casual-chic, a term that only females understand. Basically, it entails packing swimsuits, sarongs and pareos, white pants and shorts, T-shirts and short-sleeved tops, and sandals and espadrilles and leaving ample room in your bags for whatever you may buy. While the official currency is the euro, U.S. dollars are accepted everywhere. For men: bathing trunks, sports shirts, cotton trousers and shorts, and sandals or Top-Siders. Don't forget the SPF (and if you want to swim and sunbathe in the altogether, apply it to your most sensitive body parts too).

DIRECTORY

HOTELS:

Eden Rock, the oldest luxury hotel on the island, is conveniently located in St. Jean, close to the shops there and the airport and not far from the main town, Gustavia. Owners Jane and David Matthews have done a superb job of converting what was once the home-cum-shabby-chic-inn of former St. Barths' mayor, Rémy de Haenen, into a world-class property with an excellent restaurant—On the Rocks, for dinner. The open-air Sand Bar is best for breakfast and lunch. Most fun activity: watching planes land and take off. Part of the expansion was building two lavish villas, including the over-the-top Villa Rockstar, which is complete with a screening room and professional recording studio. Eden Rock's boutique is one of the nicest in St. Jean, and the art gallery, the personal project of Jane Matthews, cooperates with the New York Academy of Art to provide an artist-in-residence program.

Le Sereno was designed by Christian Liaigre, the modernist French decorator and longtime St. Barths devotee. Its thirty-seven suites and villas face the turquoise waters of the Grand Cul de Sac. The hotel's name is apt, for the setting is serene and private. Writer Malachy Duffy describes Le Sereno as Eden Rock's "aesthetic opposite." Most taxing activity: floating in the sea or the pool and watching the kite surfing and wind surfing. The hotel's restaurant, Des Pêcheurs, specializes in seafood (try the Madagascar langoustines). In addition to Liaigre, Le Sereno has partnered with French luxury linen maker B. Porthault and British handbag designer Anya Hindmarch. Latest feature: a new spa in collaboration with La Ligne St. Barth with an outdoor pavilion facing the lagoon of Grand Cul de Sac.

Opposite: Fresh grilled fish at the Hôtel Saint-Barth Isle de France.

Clockwise, from left: Tropical fruit and cocktails at the pool deck of Hôtel Le Toiny; the reception area of the spa at Hôtel Saint-Barth Isle de France; a barman gets ready to shake things up at Le Sereno hotel; lunch with a view at Le Sereno; fine dining (and fabulous scenery) at On The Rocks restaurant at the Eden Rock Hotel in St. Jean.

Above: Hôtel Guanahani & Spa near Grand Cul de Sac is legendary for its French style and glorious poolside cafe.

Hôtel Saint-Barth Isle de France: "Nantucket meets St. Tropez" is how owner Charles Vere Nicoll explains what he set out to create at his lovely secluded property on the Anse des Flamands on the island's western side. When Vere Nicoll (who is also the island's resident Anglican vicar) and his wife, Mandie, married, they spent their honeymoon at the hotel and returned so often that they finally decided to buy the place when it was available. Pluses: four-poster beds, down comforters, a color scheme of blue and white or geranium red and white. You may even encounter an iguana or two.

Hôtel Guanahani & Spa is the island's largest hotel and its only full service resort, located between the Anse de Maréchal and the reef-protected Grand Cul de Sac. Two pools, a Clarins spa, a jacuzzi, tennis courts, and water sports make this a good choice for people who don't want to just loll on the beach. Booking the Wellness Suite gives you private access to the spa after hours. The main dinner restaurant is Le Bartolomeo. L'Indigo, the poolside café, is where one can have a light and pleasant lunch. Like Eden Rock, it's a great place for families.

Above: A lobster dish at Restaurant Le Gaïac at Hôtel Le Toiny.

Hôtel Le Toiny, is the most tucked-away lodging on the island. The fifteen villa suites are surrounded by tropical vegetation. If you really want to feel remote, stay here and hide out. It is situated on a hillside on the eastern side and not on the beach. You wouldn't want to swim there anyway—too many undercurrents, which makes it a favorite of surfers. Instead, each villa has its own pool and kitchenette, and there is a Provençal motif and Le Gaïac restaurant, which, among other things, serves the best Sunday brunch on the island. If Le Toiny isn't private enough for you, rent a villa.

There are other lovely hotels and guesthouses on St. Barths that many swear by, including Les Ilets de la Plage, La Banane, Le Christopher, Le Village St Jean, Hôtel Manapany & Spa, and Tom Beach Hotel.

VILLA RENTALS

The best-known rental company is Sibarth (sibarth.com), which has been operating full-tilt and full-service since 1975. Another excellent agency is Wimco (wimco.com), headquartered in Newport, Rhode Island. (See Chapter 5.) Also reliable is St. Barths Properties (stbarth.com).

RESTAURANTS

Food is a consuming passion on St. Barths, which boasts the best in the Caribbean. In addition to the hotel restaurants, there are plenty of fine freestanding eateries to choose from. Everyone has his or her favorites, and here are a few that are mentioned regularly: Maya's, for creative Creole; the easygoing Esprit de Saline; L'Isola and PaCri, for excellent Italian food; Eddy's, for touches of Thai and Creole; Le Tamarin, for langoustines in an exotic setting; and Santa Fe, in Lurin, for barbecued fish and wraparound decks. For drinks and lighter fare: Le Select and Le Bar de l'Oubli, both in Gustavia. A great spot for cocktails overlooking Gustavia harbor is the Carl Gustaf hotel.

NIGHTCLUBS

There are several, but the best known are Nikki Beach in St. Jean, next to Eden Rock, and Le Ti St Barth in Pointe Milou.

TAKE OUT

Maya's To Go, across from the airport, and Kiki-é Mo in St. Jean.

EVENT PLANNING

Melanie Smith can be contacted at melanie.st.barths@wanadoo.fr. St-Barth Celebrations owner, Aurélie can be contacted at contact@st-barth-celebrations.com. Galen Cobb Limoges works through Wimco to plan unique occasions for her clients. Go to wimco.com for more information.

SHOPPING

In Gustavia: Ralph Lauren, Hermès, Lacoste, Cartier, and Bulgari, plus specialty shops like 100% Capri, Manuel Canovas, Lolita Jaca, Stéphane & Bernard, Jenny and Donna del Sol. For furniture and objects: Home and Christian Liaigre. St. Jean has some tasty stores too, including Christiane Celle's new eponymous boutique. Others: Clic Bookstore & Gallery; Ligne St Barth, for lotions and treatments; the products of Belou's P that are available for custom-order. Hand-woven Panama hats, an island speciality, are available on order from Wewa Design at wendystbarths@hotmail.com.

This page: Eddy's in Gustavia. *Opposite, above:* Mother and daughter Roma Marshall and Ambika Marshall, perfectly capture the island's casual-chic dress code. *Opposite, below:* Colorful sarongs at the shop at Hôtel Saint-Barth Isle de France.

Getting There's Not Always Half The Fun

Airport Gustav III's landing strip is not known as "La Tourmente" for nothing. It handles only small aircrafts, like Twin Otters and other STOLs, and planes cannot arrive or depart after dark because the airport doesn't have a system for managing instrument landings or takeoffs. The runway, only 2,170 feet long, is wedged between two hills. It takes a deft pilot to make the descent smoothly and stop the plane short of slipping into the Baie de St. Jean. Many of the planes are not exactly new, either: Yan Cor, an experienced pilot who has been flying in and out of St. Barths for years, says that the Piper Aztecs he flies were built between 1975 and 1979. When asked what he does to put nervous fliers at ease, he answers: "Joke."

Gary Topping, an aviation expert and travel agent, was general manager of Winair in the early 1970s. He has vivid memories, like the time a bag of live lobsters, brought by the pilot and stashed under the plane's backseat, came undone, permitting the lobsters to wander freely in the cabin, some of them getting caught on passengers' feet.

Goats on the runway were another problem, requiring the pilot to do a "sweep" of the runway before landing to make sure it was clear. "I went on one of these late one afternoon with two guests of David Rockefeller," Topping remembers. "After the third sweep we were finally able to land. The color of the 'Rocker' guests was somewhere between green and yellow."

Acknowledgments

Suffice it to say that any book that focuses on a place owes a debt to many of the people connected with it. *In the Spirit of St. Barths* would not have been possible without the support, generosity, and ongoing enthusiasm of the following individuals: Myron Clement and Joseph Petrocik, who helped plan my first trip there when they were doing public relations for the island and who jump-started this project; Dena Kaye, whom I visited on that trip and who introduced me to her St. Barths; Jane and David Matthews, the incredibly kind and hospitable owners of the Eden Rock, who led me to many of the people I interviewed; Maya and Randy Gurley and Christiane Celle and Antoine Verglas, who, like the Matthewses, made sure I reached some of the key players on the island; President Bruno Magras, for all that he has accomplished as a native son and statesman. Every one of these lovely folks opened doors that might otherwise have remained closed. In addition, I would like to thank Malachy Duffy, Jean Pagliuso, Rose Marie Bravo and William Jackey, Brook and Roger Lacour, Richard Fallin, Grace Leo, Sally Fischer, Ruth Schwartz, I.B. Charneau, Hélène Muntal and Franck Garcia, Richard David Story, Cindi Leive, Charles Vere Nicoll, Olivia Chantecaille and Ren Grady, Sylvie and Olivier Chantecaille, Nicole Peraud, Kino Bachellier, Melanie Smith, Javier Vila, Antonio Aiello, Colin Cowie, Geneviève Jouany, Jeanne Audy-Rowland, Alicia Bythewood, Bruce Gordon, Ellen Levine, Jeet Singh, Janis Fiori, Yan Cor, Gary Topping, Sonia Tejero, Nathalie Clifford, Gretchen and Dwight Fenton, Christian Wattiau, Anne Dental, Gary Walther, and Pier Guerci. To everyone at Assouline, I send you a huge *merci beaucoup*. Thanks finally to my assistant, Glenna MacGrotty, and my husband, Colt Givner, who've been steadfastly by my side cheering me on—for decades.

A boat belonging to the Eden Rock Hotel sets sail.

Credits

Page 4-5: © Linda Whitwam/Getty Images; page 6-7: Courtesy of Michel Hassan; page 8: © Dena Kaye/Courtesy of Pamela Fiori; page 10: © Rick Guber; page 12-13 (from left): Courtesy of Michel Hassan, courtesy of Hôtel Saint-Barth Isle de France, courtesy of the Clement-Petrocik Company; page 14-15: Photo by Slim Aarons/Hulton Archive/Getty Images; page 17: © William Abranowicz / Art + Commerce; page 18-19: Photograph by Slim Aarons and Meg O'Neil; page 20-21: © Pierre Carreau; page 22: © Melanie Acevedo; page 25: © Bridgeman Art Library; page 26: © Stanislas Defize; page 28-29 (from left): Courtesy of De Haenen family (2), Courtesy of Eden Rock Hotel; page 30: © Stanislas Defize; page 31: Photo by Roger Viollet/Getty Images; page 32: Coutesy of Bruno Magras; page 34-35: Courtesy of Colt Givner; page 37: © Jean-Philippe Piter; page 38-39: Photograph by Slim Aarons and Meg O'Neil; page 41: © Miki Duisterhof; page 43 (clockwise from top left): © Miki Duisterhof, Photo by Mark Mainz/ Getty Images, courtesy of Colt Givner; page 44: © Miki Duisterhof; page 45: © Rick Guber; page 46-47: Courtesy of Eden Rock Hotel; page 49: Courtesy of Hélène Muntal; page 50-51: Courtesy of NASA; page 52-53: Courtesy of Angelika Schubert; page 54-55: Courtesy of Olivia Chantecaille; page 56-57: Photo DigitalGlobe via Getty Images; page 58-59: © Pierre Carreau; page 60-63: © Alain Buisson; page 65: Courtesy of Colt Givner; page 66 (clockwise from top left): Courtesy of Rose Marie Bravo, © Jean Pagliuso, © Melanie Acevedo, courtesy of Christiane Celle, © Pierre Carreau, Courtesy of Kelly Bensimon; page 67: © Melanie Acevedo; page 68-69: Courtesy of Angelika Schubert; page 70-72: © Pierre Carreau; page 73: © Julie Skarratt; page 74-75: © Dianne Athey/Photo by Peter Goldman; page 76-77: © Jean Pagliuso; page 78: Courtesy of Shutterstock; page 79: © Melanie Acevedo; page 81: © William Abranowicz / Art + Commerce; page 82-83: Courtesy of Michel Hassan; page 84-85: © Jean Pagliuso; page 86-87: © Jean Pagliuso, © KCSPresse / Splash News, © Oberto Gili, © Jean Pagliuso, © Murray Andrew/ Corbis Sygma, © Jean Pagliuso, courtesy of Priscilla Rattazzi, © Jean Pagliuso (2), courtesy of the Matthews Family; page 89: © Jean Pagliuso; page 90-91: © Miki Duisterhof; page 94-95: © Jean Pagliuso; page 96: Courtesy of Eden Rock Hotel; page 97: © Jean Pagliuso; page 98: © Oberto Gili; page 100: © Pierre Carreau (top), courtesy of Priscilla Rattazzi (bottom); page 101 (clockwise from top left): Coutesy of Angelika Schubert, courtesy of Rose Marie Bravo, © Jean Pagliuso (2); page 103: Courtesy of Sibarth Villa Rentals; page 104-07: Esto / Architectural Digest / Condé Nast Archive. Copyright © Condé Nast; page 108-09: Courtesy of Sibarth Villa Rentals; page 110-11: Photo by Slim Aarons/Getty Images; page 112-13 (clockwise from top left): © Wendell Maruyama/Originally published in Vogue, © Patrick Demarchelier/Originally published in Vogue (3), © Carlyne Cerf De Dudzeele/Originally published in Vogue; 116-17: Buck / Architectural Digest / Condé Nast Archive. Copyright © Condé Nast; page 118-21: Courtesy of Sibarth Villa Rentals; page 122: © Julie Skarratt; page 125 (clockwise from top left): © Gerard Tessier, © Julie Skarratt, © Gerard Tessier, © Julie Skarratt (4), © Thayer Allyson Gowdy, © Julie Skarratt; page 128-29: © Julie Skarratt; page 131: © Thayer Allyson Gowdy; 132-33: © Miki Duisterhof; 135: Courtesy of Hôtel Saint-Barth Isle de France; page 136-37 (clockwise from top left): Courtesy of Hôtel Le Toiny, courtesy of Hôtel Saint-Barth Isle de France, courtesy of Hôtel Le Sereno (2), courtesy of Eden Rock Hotel; page 138: Courtesy of Hôtel Guanahani & Spa; page 139: Courtesy of Hôtel Le Toiny; page 140: © Miki Duisterhof; page 141: © Miki Duisterhof (top), courtesy of Colt Givner (bottom); page 142: Courtesy of Eden Rock Hotel.

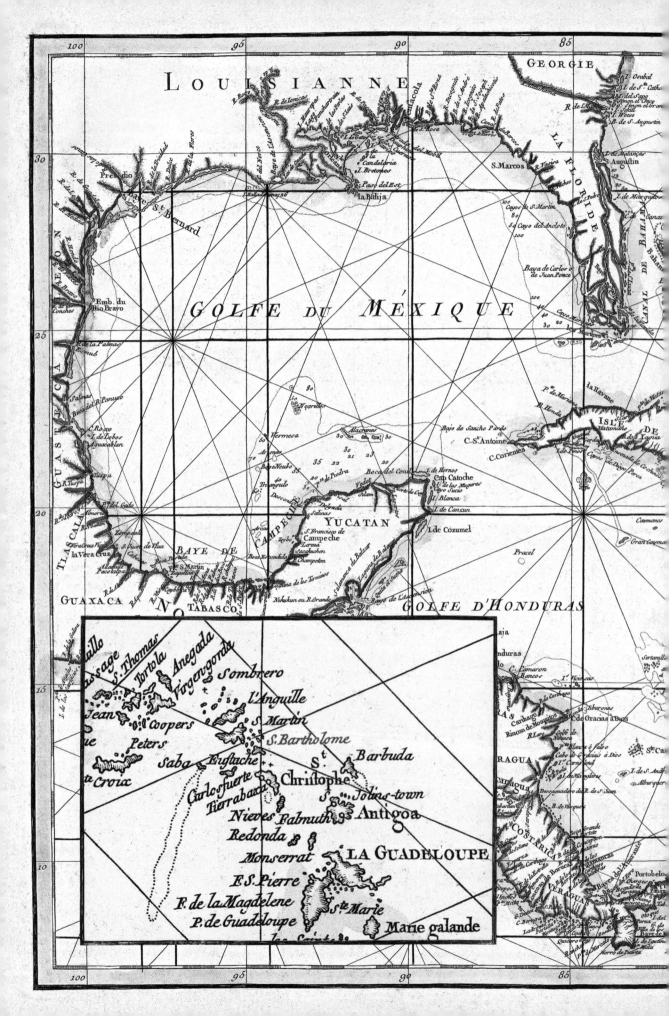